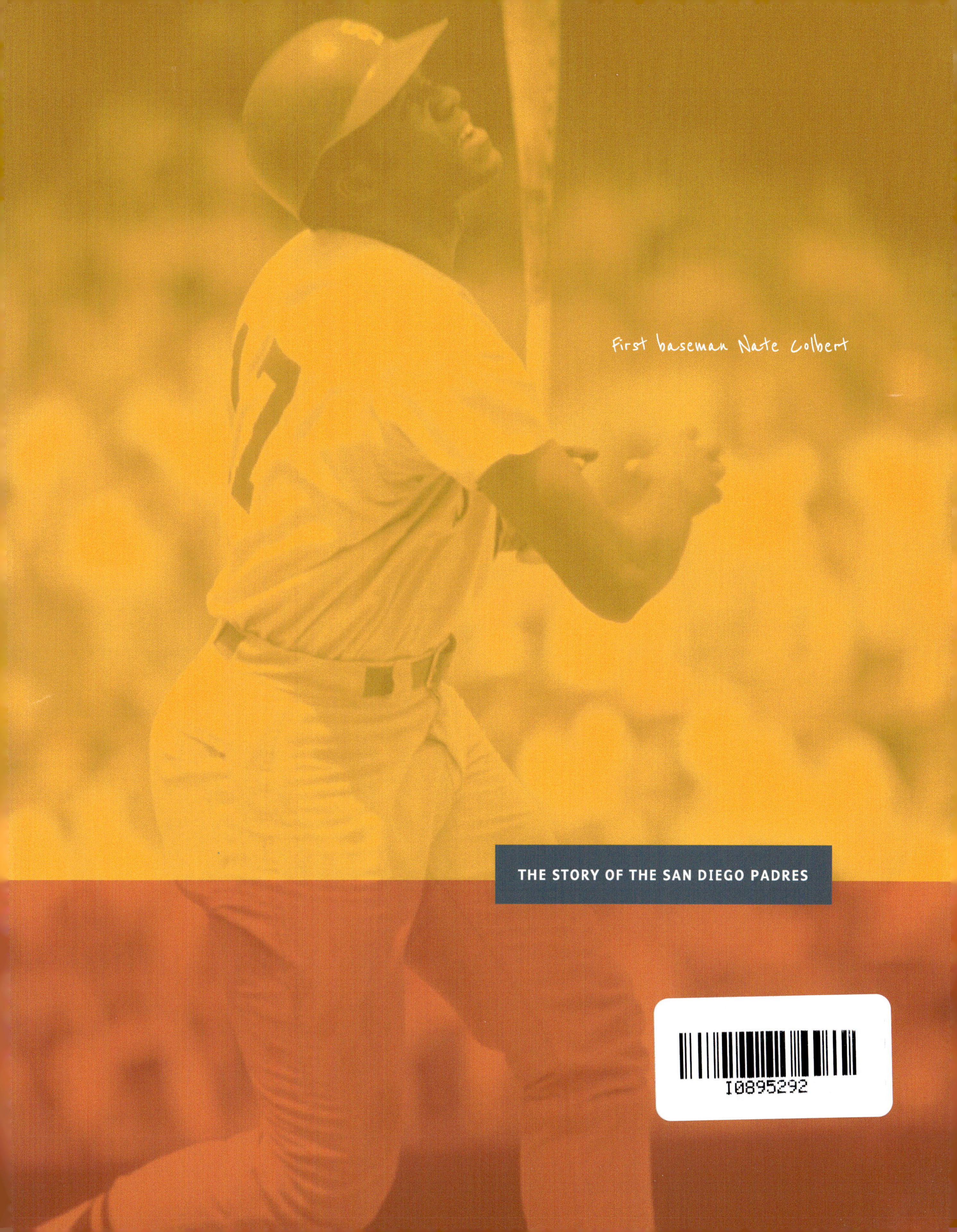

First baseman Nate Colbert

THE STORY OF THE SAN DIEGO PADRES

Third baseman Manny Machado

THE STORY OF THE

SAN DIEGO PADRES

JIM WHITING

Outfielder Brian Giles

CREATIVE SPORTS

CREATIVE EDUCATION / CREATIVE PAPERBACKS

Published by Creative Education and Creative Paperbacks
P.O. Box 227, Mankato, Minnesota 56002
Creative Education and Creative Paperbacks are imprints of The Creative Company
www.thecreativecompany.us

Book Design by Graham Morgan
Art direction by Blue Design (www.bluedes.com)

Images by Associated Press/Gregory Bull, cover, Orlando Ramirez, 10; Getty Images/Adam Glanzman, 10, Andy Hayt, 6 (top, left), 22–23, Daniel Shirey, 2, 9, 31, Diamond Images, 1, Don Smith, 3, Elsa, 7 (bottom, right), Focus On Sport, 7 (bottom, left), George Gojkovich, 15, Jed Jacobsohn, 6 (bottom, right), John R. McCutchen/Union–Tribune, 16, K.C. Alfred/San Diego Union–Trib, 26–27, Lachlan Cunningham, 30, Louis Requena, 12, Otto Greule Jr, 4–5, 32, Rich Pilling/MLB Photos, cover, 20, Rich Pilling, 19, 25, Rob Leiter, 29, Stephen Dunn, 6 (top, right), 7 (top, right), 18, Todd Warshaw, 6 (bottom, left), Tom Hauck, 7 (top, left); Unsplash/Justin Wolff, 11

Library of Congress Cataloging-in-Publication Data
Names: Whiting, Jim, 1943- author
Title: The story of the San Diego Padres / by: Jim Whiting.
Description: Mankato, Minnesota : Creative Education and Creative Paperbacks, [2026] | Series: Creative sports : Major League Baseball | Includes index. | Audience: Ages 8-12 | Audience: Grades 4-6 | Summary: "Discover the San Diego Padres' thrilling journey from their early struggles to recent playoff triumphs, featuring legendary players, dramatic moments, and the Major League Baseball team's quest for a World Series title. Written for middle-grade readers. Includes table of contents, sidebars, and index"– Provided by publisher.
Identifiers: LCCN 2025013120 (print) | LCCN 2025013121 (ebook) | ISBN 9798895811061 library binding | ISBN 9798896800590 paperback | ISBN 9798895812327 ebook
Subjects: LCSH: San Diego Padres (Baseball team : National League of Professional Baseball Clubs)–History–Juvenile literature
Classification: LCC GV875.S33 W54 2026 (print) | LCC GV875.S33 (ebook) | DDC 796.357/6409794985--dc23/eng/20250530
LC record available at https://lccn.loc.gov/2025013120
LC ebook record available at https://lccn.loc.gov/2025013121

Printed in the United States

First baseman Adrián González

Padres

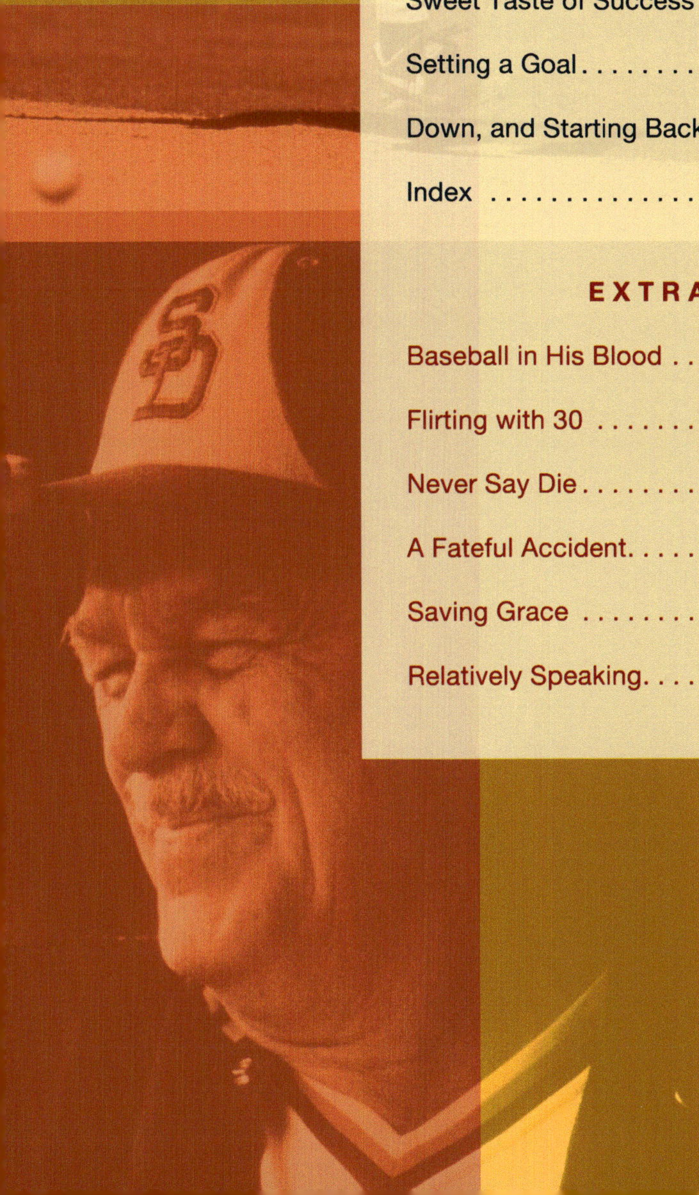

CONTENTS

EXTRA INNINGS

SLAM DIEGO

The 2020 Major League Baseball (MLB) season got off to a late start because of the COVID-19 pandemic. So when the San Diego Padres faced the Texas Rangers on August 17, they had played just 23 games.

In the top of the seventh inning, Padres shortstop Fernando Tatis Jr. smacked a three-run home run. An inning later, he came up with the bases loaded. He ran the count to three balls, no strikes. Manager Jayce Tingler gave Tatis the "take" sign. That means that no matter where the next pitch was, Tatis wasn't supposed to swing. If the pitch were a ball, he would earn a base on balls and force in a run. If it were a strike, Tatis would still be ahead in the count. He would probably get a good pitch to hit.

Tatis didn't see the sign. Instead, he swung and hit an opposite-field home run into the right field seats. That gave him seven runs batted in (RBIs) for the game. His two homers sparked a 14–4 San Diego win.

The two teams played the following day. With two outs, Tatis and two other Padres loaded the bases. Right fielder Wil Myers hit a grand slam. It was the second slam of his

Shortstop Fernando Tatis Jr.

EXTRA INNINGS

FERNANDO TATIS JR.
SHORTSTOP, RIGHT FIELD
PADRES SEASONS: 2019–PRESENT
HEIGHT: 6-FOOT-3
WEIGHT: 217 POUNDS
KEY STATS: .279 BATTING AVERAGE, 127 HOME RUNS, 332 RBIS, 2X ALL-STAR

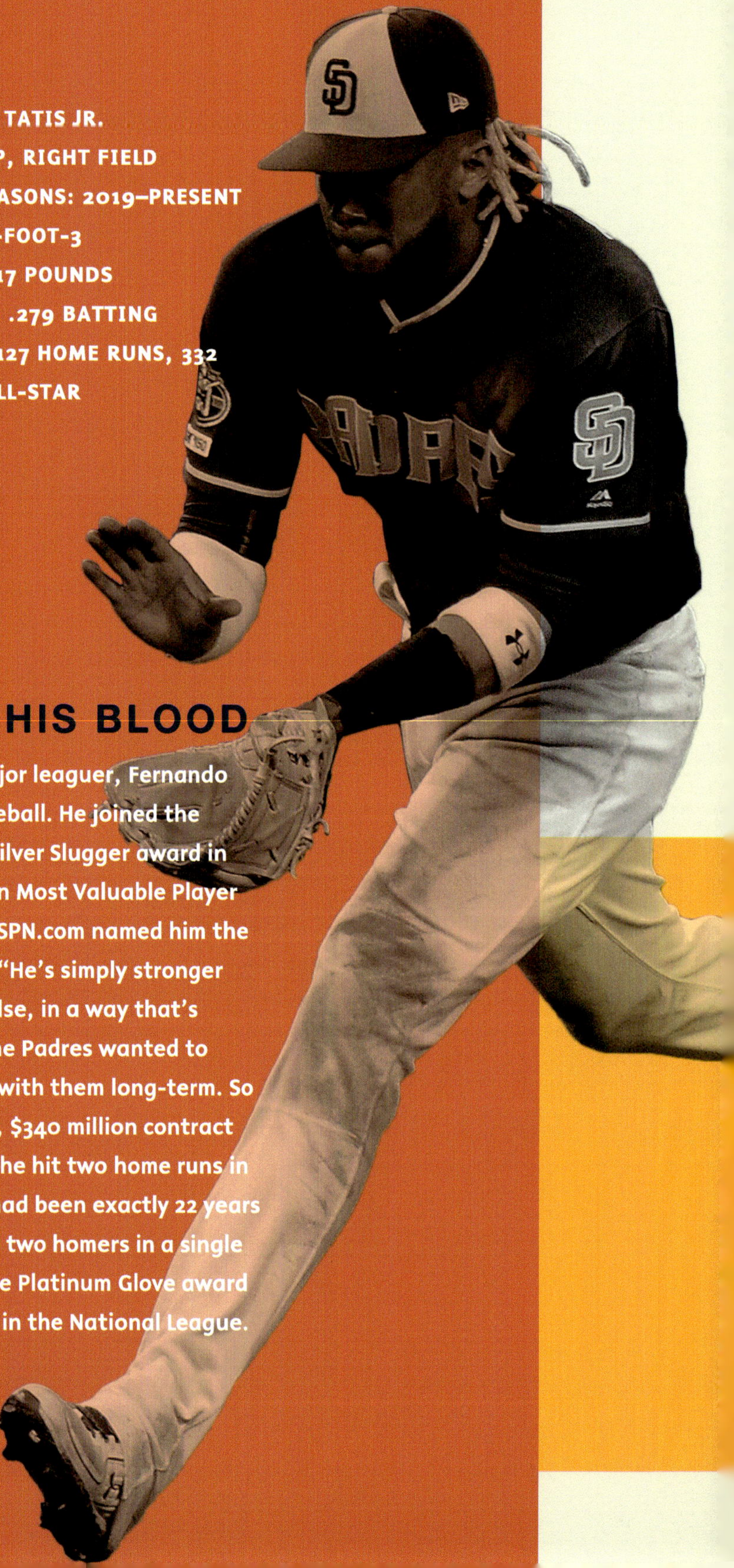

BASEBALL IN HIS BLOOD

Because his father was a major leaguer, Fernando Tatis Jr. grew up around baseball. He joined the Padres in 2019. He won the Silver Slugger award in 2020 while finishing fourth in Most Valuable Player (MVP) voting. Sam Miller of ESPN.com named him the most exciting player in MLB. “He’s simply stronger and faster than everybody else, in a way that’s quickly visible,” he wrote. The Padres wanted to make sure that he would be with them long-term. So they signed him to a 14-year, $340 million contract extension. In a coincidence, he hit two home runs in a game on April 23, 2021. It had been exactly 22 years since his father had swatted two homers in a single inning. In 2023, Tatis won the Platinum Glove award as the best defensive player in the National League.

San Diego skyline

career. The first one came seven years earlier and was also his first career home run. The Padres won 6–4.

The teams faced off again on August 19. The game was tied 2–2 after nine innings. The Rangers pushed across a run in the top of the 10th. With one out and the bases loaded, San Diego third baseman Manny Machado came to the plate. Nine days earlier, he had hit a grand slam against the Los Angeles Dodgers. He did the same thing that night. His blast was one of MLB's most dramatic plays: a walkoff home run. It gave San Diego a 6–3 victory. It was just the fourth time in MLB history that a team had hit grand slams in three consecutive games.

The next day, first baseman Eric Hosmer came up in the fifth inning with the bases loaded and one out. Hosmer hit a drive to right field that barely cleared the fence. It was the first time that a team had hit grand slams in four straight games! San Diego won 8–7 to sweep the four-game series. "We were kind of talking about it before the game, just how amazing three was in three games," Hosmer said. "It's fun to be a part of history."

It seemed fitting that Tatis and Machado were two of the runners on base when Hosmer hit his record-breaking slam. Their homers had set the stage

SD

for the new record. It seemed especially fitting that Tatis kicked off the slam parade and was a part of the next three. His father Fernando Tatis Sr. is the only MLB player to hit two grand slams in a single inning. He accomplished the feat in 1999. His eight RBIs in a single inning are also an MLB record.

TEAM ON A MISSION

In 1969, four new MLB teams began playing. One was in San Diego. It was in the National League (NL) West Division. San Diego had hosted minor-league teams since 1936. Those teams were all named the Padres. The name honored the churchmen who founded California's first Catholic mission in 1769. The new MLB franchise inherited the Padres name. It also inherited the strong fan base of the minor-league club.

The Padres went just 52–110 in their first season. No starter hit above .264. Fans cheered for two young stars. Cito Gaston was a smooth-swinging outfielder, and Nate Colbert was a hard-hitting first baseman. They helped the Padres improve to 63 wins in 1970. Unfortunately, that was the high mark for several years. The offense never seemed to supply enough runs to win consistently.

As the losses mounted, fans stopped attending. Owner C. Arnholt Smith sold the team. The new owners wanted to relocate the Padres to the nation's capital in Washington, D.C., before the 1974 season. The team's equipment was packed for the cross-country move. Baseball cards showed San Diego players in Washington. Then Ray Kroc stepped in. The wealthy businessman had built McDonalds into the world's most successful fast-food franchise. He

Right fielder Dave Winfield

purchased the team and kept it in San Diego. Grateful fans thronged San Diego Stadium's turnstiles. Attendance surpassed one million for the first time.

By the mid-1970s, the team had two rising stars. One was right fielder Dave Winfield from the University of Minnesota. Winfield was drafted by teams from four professional leagues: National Basketball Association, American Basketball Association, National Football League, and MLB. He never played in the minors. He went straight from college to the majors. He would go on to a Baseball Hall of Fame career. Though he played for five other teams, he wore a Padres cap when he was inducted. He wanted to honor the team and the city where he got his start.

The other one was pitcher Randy Jones. His best pitch was a sinkerball that led many hitters to ground out. "I didn't throw hard enough to break a pane of glass," he joked. In 1975, Jones became the team's first 20-game winner. He topped the major leagues with 22 wins in 1976. He earned the Cy Young Award that year. Fireballing Rookie of the Year Butch Metzger added 11 more victories. The Padres won 73 games.

In 1978, San Diego posted its first winning season with an 84–78 record. Wily starter Gaylord Perry joined the team through a trade. He won 21 games and captured the Cy Young Award. Ace reliever Rollie Fingers saved 37 games. Dazzling rookie shortstop Ozzie Smith and speedy left fielder Gene Richards added youthful exuberance.

The Padres had high hopes for 1979. Yet poor pitching and injuries doomed the club. It suffered another losing season.

Winfield and Jones were gone after the 73–89 1980 season. Smith left the following year. The changes destroyed the team's budding chemistry. Kroc hired Dick Williams as manager. Williams had piloted the Oakland Athletics to back-to-back world championships in the early 1970s. He promised to get the Padres on the winning track.

EXTRA INNINGS

RANDY JONES
PITCHER
PADRES SEASONS: 1973–80
HEIGHT: 6-FOOT-0
WEIGHT: 170 POUNDS
KEY STATS: 92–105 WIN-LOSS RECORD, 3.30 EARNED RUN AVERAGE, 677 STRIKEOUTS, 2X ALL-STAR

FLIRTING WITH 30

Just after the halfway point of the 1976 season, Randy Jones had a record of 16 wins, 3 losses. *Sports Illustrated* magazine put him on the cover of the July 12 issue with the headline, "Threat to Win 30." Between 1901 and 1934, only 12 pitchers had won at least 30 games in a single season. Fans flocked to the stadium when Jones pitched. But he was involved in a car crash in August. His teammates didn't provide much run support, either. He finished with 22 wins. Just before the end of the season, he suffered an arm injury that eventually forced him to retire. Jones remains a San Diego icon. Kevin Kernan of ballnine.com called him "the greatest baseball ambassador the Padres could have, promoting the game and his foundation does meaningful work."

CHICAGO CUBS VS.
SAN DIEGO PADRES
NATIONAL LEAGUE
CHAMPIONSHIP SERIES
OCTOBER 2–7, 1984

NEVER SAY DIE

The Cubs won the first two games in Chicago. Yet more than 15,000 fans turned out to greet the Padres when they returned home. "It was crazy," said outfielder Tony Gwynn. "We're on the verge of getting swept out of the playoffs, and the fans came out to welcome us." The Padres rode that momentum to a 7–1 victory in Game 3. Game 4 was tied 5–5 going into the bottom of the tenth. With one out and Gwynn at first, first baseman Steve Garvey sent the ball over the 370-foot mark in center field for a walkoff two-run home run! The San Diego Union Tribune called it the greatest moment in San Diego sports history. Chicago took a quick 3–0 lead in Game 5. San Diego scored two runs in the sixth inning and four in the seventh to take a 6–3 lead. Goose Gossage shut down the Cubs in the last two innings. It was the first time that a team had won the NLCS after trailing two games.

SWEET TASTE OF SUCCESS

The Padres began the 1982 season with a new attitude. "[Manager] Dick [Williams] told us at the beginning that team play was in and excuses were out," catcher Terry Kennedy said. "If you produced, you played. Simple as that." The team bought into that message. It set a new franchise record with an 11-game winning streak. Outfielder Tony Gwynn was called up from the minor leagues in July. He collected two hits in his first game. It was a sign of things to come. The Padres finished the season 81–81. They matched that mark in 1983. Even better times lay ahead.

The Padres brought in several veteran stars before the 1984 season. First baseman Steve Garvey had been a perennial All-Star with the Los Angeles Dodgers. San Diego also added slick-fielding third baseman Graig Nettles and closer Rich "Goose" Gossage. The newcomers joined pitching standouts Eric Show and Ed Whitson. The Padres finally had talent at the plate and on the mound. Williams told reporters, "We're ready."

He was right. San Diego won the division by a 12-game margin. Gwynn led the majors with 213 hits. He won the first of his eight NL batting crowns. Garvey did not commit a single error in the field. The Padres headed to the playoffs for the first time in their 15-year existence. They defeated the Chicago Cubs in the National League Championship Series (NLCS). The team moved on to the World Series against the Detroit Tigers. Detroit overpowered the Padres, four games to one. Still, San Diego fans looked forward to the next season.

Catcher Benito Santiago

The 1985 Padres featured seven All-Stars. But the team slipped to third in the division. Williams left. The team suffered through losing campaigns in 1986 and 1987. The 1988 Padres got back on the winning track with an 83–78 record. They were led by Gwynn, catcher Benito Santiago, and switch-hitting second baseman Roberto Alomar. San Diego started slowly in 1989. On August 19, it was just 60–63. Then they went 19–8 in September and finished 89–73. They missed the postseason by just three games.

San Diego emerged as an offensive powerhouse in the early 1990s. Two heavy hitters, third baseman Gary Sheffield and first baseman Fred "Crime Dog" McGriff, joined Gwynn in the lineup. Soon, the NL began to notice the slugging Padres. After one game against San Diego, Pittsburgh Pirates manager Jim Leyland muttered, "They gotta break these guys up. They just wore my pitching staff out."

Pitcher Rich "Goose" Gossage

EXTRA INNINGS

TONY GWYNN
RIGHT FIELD
PADRES SEASONS: 1982–2001
HEIGHT: 5-FOOT-11
WEIGHT: 185 POUNDS
KEY STATS: .338 BATTING AVERAGE, 135 HOME RUNS, 1,138 RBIS, 15X ALL-STAR

A FATEFUL ACCIDENT

Tony Gwynn was a high school sensation in basketball and baseball. San Diego State University recruited him as a basketball point guard. He didn't play baseball as a freshman to concentrate on basketball. The following season, two SDSU baseball outfielders were hit by a car while riding their bikes and seriously injured. Baseball coach Jim Dietz scrambled to replace them. One of his infielders, Bobby Meacham, had played baseball against Gwynn and recommended him. Dietz invited Gwynn to try out even though he had never heard of him. He made the team. The Padres took him in the third round of the 1981 MLB Draft. He played his entire 20-year career in San Diego. He was a 15-time All-Star and won eight NL batting titles. "Fate is involved in everyone's life," said Dietz. "If Tony hadn't played college baseball, he wouldn't have been seen by major-league scouts ... We're talking about a career that likely wouldn't have happened."

SETTING A GOAL

The Padres recorded winning seasons in 1991 and 1992. They slipped back in the standings in the following two years. In 1995, the Padres added center fielder Steve Finley and hard-nosed third baseman Ken Caminiti. They fired up their teammates with their on-field intensity. Both won Gold Glove awards.

The team set a lofty goal for 1996. They wanted to reach the playoffs for the first time since 1984. The Padres engaged the Dodgers in a heated battle for the NL West title. It came down to the last three games of the season. San Diego won all three. It took the division crown. Unfortunately, the team could not carry that momentum into the playoffs. St. Louis Cardinals swept the National League Division Series (NLDS) in three games.

Still, it had been an amazing year. The team had a 21-game improvement over 1995. The dramatic turnaround earned Bruce Bochy NL Manager of the Year honors. Caminiti smacked 40 home runs and 130 RBIs. He earned the NL Most Valuable Player (MVP) award. Gwynn captured his seventh NL batting title and played in his 12th All-Star Game. Finley won another Gold Glove award.

Two years later, the Padres won a franchise-record 98 games. They took the NL West crown. Left fielder Greg Vaughn slammed 50 home runs. Reliable closer Trevor Hoffman notched 53 saves. In the NLDS, the Padres defeated the Houston Astros. They overcame the Atlanta Braves in a tense, six-game NLCS. After 14 years, San Diego was back in the "Fall Classic."

Right fielder Dave Winfield

The Padres faced off against the New York Yankees. Vaughn slammed two home runs in the first game. Gwynn added a third. It wasn't enough. The Yankees stormed back to win the game. New York won the next three games as well to sweep the series.

Before the 1999 season, Caminiti and Finley became free agents. They left San Diego. Several other key players were traded away. Gwynn stayed. He knocked his 3,000th career hit on August 6. In a remarkable coincidence, he had notched his 2,000th hit on the same date six years earlier.

But the team mustered just 74 wins. Hard-hitting third baseman Phil Nevin sparked the offense in 2000 and 2001. He hit over .300 both times. Unfortunately, injuries and mediocre play plagued the Padres. Gwynn hung up his spikes after the 2001 season. His departure seemed to deflate the team's spirits. They went just 66–96 and 64–98 in the next two seasons.

By 2004, San Diego seemed poised to bounce back. Pitcher Jake Peavy led the majors with an earned run average (ERA) of 2.27. He struck out 173 batters. Though they barely missed the playoffs, the team compiled an 87–75 record. The 2005 and 2006 seasons were almost mirror images of each other. The Padres won the NL West both times. It was the first time with back-to-back playoff appearances. But St. Louis bounced them in the NLDS both times.

Pitcher Jake Peavy

TREVOR HOFFMAN

PITCHER

PADRES SEASONS: 1993–2008

HEIGHT: 6-FOOT-1

WEIGHT: 200 POUNDS

KET STATS: 54–64 WIN-LOSS RECORD, 552 SAVES, 2.76 EARNED RUN AVERAGE, 6X ALL-STAR

EXTRA INNINGS

SAVING GRACE

At just six weeks old, Trevor Hoffman had a damaged kidney removed. He couldn't play contact sports. So he turned to baseball. He became a shortstop. The Cincinnati Reds took him in the 11th round of the 1989 MLB Draft. Hoffman struggled with his hitting in his first year in the minor leagues. His manager converted him to a pitcher because he had a strong arm. His 95-mile-per-hour fastball made him a successful reliever when he moved to the majors in 1993. But a shoulder injury in 1994 necessitated a new pitch. Hoffman found it with a devastating change-up. In 1998, his 53 saves were the most in MLB. Counting his two final years with the Milwaukee Brewers, Hoffman saved a total of 601 games. Only Mariano Rivera of the New York Yankees, with 652, has more.

DOWN, AND STARTING BACK UP

Near the end of the 2007 season, San Diego had a slight lead for the NL Wild Card berth. But they lost the final three games. Their season was over. Peavy won the NL pitching Triple Crown. He had the lowest ERA (2.54), the most wins (19), and the most strikeouts (240). He was an easy choice for the Cy Young Award.

Over the next three years, the Padres made big changes. They tried to improve the team while reducing payroll. The new crew powered San Diego to a 90–72 record in 2010. It was the fourth-best mark in team history. But the Padres continued to fall short of the playoffs.

San Diego had losing records in the next nine seasons. But help was on the way.

After the 2018 season, San Diego had signed four-time All-Star third baseman Manny Machado to a 10-year, $300 million contract as a free agent. It was the largest free agent contract in American sports history at the time.

The Padres celebrated their 50th anniversary in 2019. The players supplied their own fireworks on May 25. They bashed seven home runs against the Toronto Blue Jays. But the Padres could not avoid yet another losing season. They finished 70–92. Machado had 32 home runs. Rookie shortstop Fernando Tatís Jr. added another 22 in just 84 games.

San Diego broke their nine-season losing streak in 2020. They finished 37–23 as the COVID-19 pandemic shortened the season. But the Dodgers swept them 3–0 in the NLDS.

Pitcher Trevor Hoffman

SAN DIEGO PADRES AT
MILWAUKEE BREWERS
SEPTEMBER 29, 2007

RELATIVELY SPEAKING

San Diego needed to defeat the Milwaukee Brewers in one of the season's two final games to secure the NL Wild Card berth. In the first of those games, the Padres clung to a 3–2 lead in the bottom of the ninth. Tony Gwynn's son Tony Jr. played for the Brewers. He faced San Diego ace reliever Trevor Hoffman as a pinch hitter with two outs and a runner on second. Hoffman was Tony Jr.'s uncle. Growing up, Tony Jr. spent countless hours with Hoffman. They talked about baseball. Hoffman explained how he pitched. So Tony Jr. had a pretty good idea what Hoffman might throw him in this situation. Using that knowledge, he slapped a two-strike triple. It tied the score. The Padres lost in extra innings. They lost the next day as well. That loss tied them with the Colorado Rockies for the Wild Card spot. The Rockies won the playoff game, 9–8. "It's kind of awkward," Tony Jr. said. "You grow up rooting for the Padres your whole entire life, and now you're in a situation where you can possibly hurt their chances getting into the playoffs."

SAN DIEG
21

Pitcher Dylan Cease

After missing the playoffs in 2021, the Padres returned in 2022. They won the NL Wild Card series and the NLDS. But the Philadelphia Phillies dominated them in the NLCS, four games to one.

Their 82–80 mark in 2023 fell short of the playoffs. Pitcher Blake Snell had a 2.25 ERA and 14 wins en route to winning the Cy Young Award.

The Padres bounced back in 2024, finishing 93–69. It was their best record since 1998. They defeated the Braves in the Wild Card series. They won two of the first three games against the Dodgers in the NLDS. But the Dodgers shut them out in the next two games to take the series.

There was one consolation. In their first 61 seasons, San Diego had been in the playoffs just five times. They won only three series during that time. In the five seasons between 2020 and 2024, they had three playoff appearances. They won four series.

For years, the Padres have brought baseball pride and professionalism to San Diego. Based in a city that started as a religious mission, the Padres have succeeded in their own mission to entertain fans. Those fans would like nothing more than to see their team bring home its first World Series title.

Second baseman Jake Cronenworth

INDEX